Let's eat, Grandma!

Karina Law

Illustrated by
Mike Phillips

W

FRANKLIN WATTS
LONDON•SYDNEY

How do grammar and punctuation help?

Grammar is a set of "rules" that humans have developed to help organise words and make ourselves understood.

Punctuation is a set of symbols that we use to guide readers through written or printed words.

Grammar and punctuation "rules" have evolved over thousands of years; the way we use language changes to adapt to our ever-changing world. Each generation adds new words and new ways of using words, keeping language exciting and fresh.

How we use language often depends on who we are communicating with, and for what purpose. But it is worth investigating how we put words and sentences together so that we can communicate with confidence.

Franklin Watts
First published in Great Britain in 2015
by The Watts Publishing Group

Text © Karina Law 2015
Illustrations © The Watts Publishing Group 2015

The author has asserted her rights in accordance with the Copyright, Designs and Patents Act, 1988.

All rights reserved.

Written by Karina Law
Illustrations by Mike Phillips
Designed by Matt Lilly
Cover design by Cathryn Gilbert

Every attempt has been made to clear copyright. Should there be any inadvertent omission please apply to the publisher for rectification.

Dewey number: 428.2
HB ISBN 978 14451 4200 5
Library ebook ISBN 978 1 4452 4202 9

Printed in China

MIX
Paper from responsible sources
FSC® C104740

Franklin Watts
An imprint of
Hachette Children's Group
Part of The Watts Publishing Group
Carmelite House
50 Victoria Embankment
London EC4Y 0DZ

An Hachette UK Company
www.hachette.co.uk
www.franklinwatts.co.uk

# Contents

Fluffy

Fang

Punctuation

Capital letters

A capital letter is used at the start of every sentence. Sometimes it is called an uppercase letter.

Capital letters have lots of other uses, too.

The personal pronoun 'I' is always a capital letter.

What's the capital of France?

F

The main words in a title often begin with a capital letter.

They are used at the start of names and places.

A capital letter is often used to begin each line in a poem.

Tiger, tiger, burning bright
In the forests of the night...

Capital letters can also be used to emphasise something of importance.

Did you know?

Some people consider it bad manners to send emails or text messages using only capital letters as IT CAN SEEM AS IF YOU ARE SHOUTING!

Sentence punctuation

A capital letter shows where a sentence begins, but there are several different punctuation marks to show where a sentence ends. It all depends on the type of sentence.

Full stops .

Most sentences end with a full stop. Full stops signal the main pauses in a piece of text. They are checkpoints at which the reader has a chance to take in what they have just read before moving on to the next sentence.

Reading is trickier when there are no full stops to guide the reader.

birds rarely argue this is because they build their nests in tall trees if you lived in a tree you wouldn't want to fall out either

Birds rarely argue. This is because they build their nests in tall trees. If you lived in a tree, you wouldn't want to fall out either.

A full stop is sometimes used in an abbreviation (shortened word or phrase).

Capt.	Captain
Nov.	November
etc.	et cetera (Latin) meaning 'and so on'
a.m.	ante meridiem (Latin) meaning 'before midday'
e.g.	exempli gratia (Latin) meaning 'for example'
i.e.	id est (Latin) meaning 'that is'

Did you know?

Traditionally, a full stop is not used for abbreviations that are contractions.

Dr (Doctor)

Mr (Mister)

Ltd (Limited)

Different people punctuate abbreviations in different ways. As time goes on, full stops are being used less and less in abbreviations.

Question marks ?

Some sentences are questions.
A question always ends with a question mark.

Questions often start with a 'question word'.

Why did the granny cross the road?

How? What? When? Where? Who? Why? Which?

Exclamation marks !

Come down!

An exclamation mark can be used at the end of a command, to give the words greater emphasis or to show that the speaker is shouting.

It can also be used to show strong emotion such as excitement, happiness, anger, shock or surprise.
Hey! Ouch! Wow! Go away!

Why are you always shouting?

?

Stop questioning me!

!

Break it up, guys...

•••

I'll put a stop to this.

•

Ellipses ...
(singular: ellipsis)

An ellipsis is a series of three dots often used to show missing words.

It can also be used at the end of an unfinished sentence. Ellipses are great for when you want to end on a cliffhanger, leaving the reader wondering what will happen next...

Commas ,

Commas are useful for separating items in lists.

> I was given slippers, chocolates, a jigsaw, soap and a cardigan for my birthday.

No comma is needed before the 'and' at the end of the list.

What's missing here?

> I like baking my budgie and computer games.

Commas are also used to separate adjectives in a descriptive sentence.

> I'm knitting a warm, fluffy, pink scarf.

Extra information is sometimes contained within a pair of commas.

> The girl, who was often late, ran quickly through the school gates.

A single comma is sometimes needed after an adverbial, a phrase or a clause. It reminds the reader to take a pause when reading.

> When I was a little girl, I liked catching butterflies.

> What's the difference between a cat and a comma? One has claws at the end of its paws; the other is a pause at the end of a clause.

Punctuation: the extra bits

Brackets, dashes, colons and semi-colons make great emoticons.

But these handy punctuation marks have another function:
they help to organise extra information.

Brackets ( )

Brackets can be used to separate information from
the rest of a sentence. They always come in pairs.

> **The Battle of Hastings (1066) was won by William
> of Normandy (William the Conqueror).**
>
> **I hoped I would get a new bike for my birthday (my old bike was stolen)
> but I wasn't sure if Mum could afford one.**

If you take the words or numbers inside a pair of brackets away,
the rest of the sentence should still make sense.

Another name for brackets is 'parentheses'. (But 'brackets' is easier to spell!)

Dashes –

A single dash can be used in a similar
way to a comma, semi-colon or colon,
indicating a pause in a sentence.

A pair of dashes can be used
in the same way as a pair of
brackets or commas – to separate
extra information from the rest
of a sentence.

> **I don't know why
> she swallowed
> a fly – perhaps
> she'll die!**

> **She wasn't like the other teachers
> – pink spiky hair, cool clothes, a
> 'black belt' in Judo – but she was
> the best teacher we ever had.**

Brackets, dashes or commas?

Brackets, dashes and commas can all be used to separate an extra piece of information from the rest of a sentence. The extra information within the brackets, dashes or commas is sometimes described as 'in parenthesis'. Different readers and writers have different preferences for using brackets, dashes or commas. Notice how other writers use them and think about the different effects they achieve. Take care not to overuse them as some readers find this annoying.

Colons :

A colon is a handy punctuation mark that makes announcements and introduces things.

A colon can be used to introduce a list.

> Please bring the following items to camp: sleeping bag, a change of clothes, towel, pyjamas, toothbrush.

Colons are often used in play scripts.

> HAMLET: To be, or not to be – that is the question.

A colon is sometimes used to introduce speech.

> The coach said: "Anyone who is not wearing the correct kit will not be allowed to take part."

Semi-colons ;

A semi-colon is a fancy punctuation mark you can use between two closely related statements instead of a full stop or a conjunction (see page 33). Using a semi-colon shows the reader that the two statements are linked in some way.

Compare different ways of separating these statements:

> **You had an enormous pizza for lunch. I had a small sandwich.**
> (Two statements separated by a full stop.)

> **You had an enormous pizza for lunch whereas I had a small sandwich.**
> (Two statements separated by a conjunction.)

> **You had an enormous pizza for lunch; I had a small sandwich.**
> (Two statements separated by a semi-colon.)

Each example is grammatically correct. The conjunction 'whereas' makes it clear that a comparison is being made. The semi-colon shows that the two statements are closely related. Both help the text to flow smoothly, avoiding the jolt of a full stop between the two related sentences.

Did you know?

Semi-colons are also useful for separating items in a list, particularly when commas alone might be confusing.

The star players were: Finn, Ethan and Hayden in the blue team; Ivy in the yellow team; Jamilla in the green team; Kamal, Jake and Ali in the red team.

Inverted commas " "

Inverted commas are used to punctuate direct speech. The inverted commas, which can also be called 'speech marks', go at the beginning and end of spoken words.

> **"That's one small step for a man, one giant leap for mankind,"**
> **said Neil Armstrong as he stepped onto the moon.**

Single or double inverted commas can be used to punctuate speech, so long as you stick to whichever you have chosen: be consistent.

> **'Reach for the stars!'** or **"Reach for the stars!"**

Spot the difference...

Inverted commas are not needed for indirect (reported) speech.

> **"Let's fly a kite," said Grandma.** (direct speech)
> **Grandma suggested that we fly a kite.** (indirect speech)

Things to watch out for:

Inverted commas are not needed before and after every sentence – only at the beginning and end of a piece of speech.

"Let's go into town." "We could watch a film!" said Betty.

"Let's go into town. We could watch a film!" said Betty.

If you interrupt a bit of speech to show who is speaking, remember to end and begin again with speech marks.

> "If you don't stop bouncing on the bed," said Mum, "you will fall and bump your head!"

Inverted commas can also be used to punctuate quotations or titles of stories, songs or poems.

Shakespeare wrote: "Neither a borrower nor a lender be."

In printed books, italics are used for the titles of books, TV shows, plays or films.

I am reading *Treasure Island* by Robert Louis Stevenson.

Apostrophes '

Apostrophes look like flying commas.

They are busy punctuation marks with two main jobs:

- **to show missing letters in a word (omission)**
- **to show who owns what (possession)**

Apostrophes: omission

When we speak, we often squash words together, omitting (missing out) some letters. We call these words 'contractions'.

In writing, an apostrophe is needed when you combine words to make a contraction. Usually, the apostrophe shows where letters are missing.

did not ⟶ **didn't**   **she is** ⟶ **she's**   **they have** ⟶ **they've**

Watch out for this common contraction as it is irregular:

will not ⟶ **won't**

Contractions can make your writing sound less formal. They can help make dialogue (conversations) sound more natural.

> **"Sorry I am late! It is not my fault – my car would not start."**
> **"Sorry I'm late! It's not my fault – my car wouldn't start."**

Watch out for:

could've
would've
should've

Remember that these are contractions. When spoken aloud, they sometimes sound like 'could of', 'would of', 'should of'. But the second word is 'have' not 'of'. An apostrophe is used to show the missing letters.

Apostrophes: possession

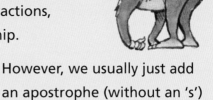

As well as showing missing letters in contractions, apostrophes can be used to show ownership.

We add **'s** after most singular nouns to show ownership of something.

> **Grandma's cat**
> **The cat's dinner**
> **The donkey's tail**
> **The monkey's bottom**

However, we usually just add an apostrophe (without an 's') after a plural noun.

> **The ladies' meeting**
> **The teachers' car park**
> **The wizards' convention**
> **The lions' enclosure**

Spot the difference...

The elephants' trunks

The elephant's trunks

For an irregular plural (one that does not end in 's') we add **'s**.

> **The children's party**
> **The men's changing room**

Take care not to overuse this busy punctuation mark! Don't add an apostrophe to plural words that end in 's' unless you are showing ownership of something.

Hyphens –

A hyphen is a punctuation mark used to link words or parts of words.

Lots of compound adjectives can be created in this way.

sugar-free   ruby-red
up-to-date
eco-friendly   short-sighted

A hyphen is shorter than a dash and there is no space before or after it.

Goodbye, hyphen – gotta dash!

Sometimes a hyphen can remove confusion.

Spot the difference...

man-eating shark   **man eating shark**

The hyphen in 'man-eating' changes the words 'man' and 'eating' into a compound adjective.

Hyphens can also be used when you can't quite fit a word on one line and you need to continue it on the next line. Make sure you only break a word after a syllable.

Compound words

Compound words are words that have been made by joining smaller words together. Most compound nouns do not need hyphens.

> **lighthouse   rattlesnake
> blueberry   toothbrush   quicksand
> toenail   download   grasshopper
> firefighter   sunflower
> skateboard   breakfast**

The meaning of a compound word is usually clear from the smaller parts. A toothbrush, for example, is a brush you use to clean your teeth.

This is not always the case.

earwig

buttercup

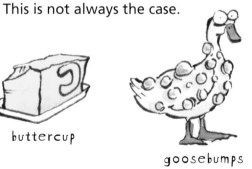

goosebumps

toadstool

Lots of jokes are based on compound words.

What do you get if you cross a snowman with a vampire?

Frostbite.

Word classes

Nouns

Humans have always found it useful to name the things around them.

These naming words are nouns.

Nouns can be divided into two groups: common nouns and proper nouns.

Common nouns

Common nouns are the ordinary names for people, places, animals and things. For example: boy, river, meerkat. Nouns can be **countable** or **non-countable**. For example: you can count strawberries but you can't count jam.

Some common nouns name things we cannot see or touch. These are known as abstract nouns.

Grammar detective

How to spot a common noun...

If you can use a, an or the in front of a word, it is probably a common noun.

peace

love

happiness

Collective nouns are names given to a group. Some of these are very familiar, such as a **band** of musicians, a **choir** of singers, a **herd** of cows, a **deck** of cards or a **flock** of birds.

Others are less well known...

knot of toads

parliament of owls

pandemonium of parrots

army of caterpillars

ambush of tigers

wisdom of wombats

sleuth of bears

murder of crows

lounge of lizards

Proper nouns

Proper nouns are specific names for people, places, brands, organisations, festivals, days of the week, months and pets.

Don't Forget!
Proper nouns always begin with a CAPITAL LETTER: Friday, January, Dan, Barcelona, Diwali.

Fluffy

Fang

Pronouns

Pronouns can be used in place of nouns.   it him I you me her we us they them he she

Pronouns help us avoid repetition.

Spot the difference...

When Billy got stuck up a tree, Billy had to be rescued by the window cleaner.

When Billy got stuck up a tree, he had to be rescued by the window cleaner.

When using pronouns, it is important to be clear about which noun the pronoun is standing in for.

Keep that dog out of the house; it's full of fleas!

Stay out of the house, Buster; it's full of fleas!

Don't Forget!

When you use the letter 'i' as a pronoun, in place of your name, it needs to be a capital 'I'.

Possessive pronouns

Possessive pronouns show that
something belongs to someone.

theirs **yours** hers
mine its ours his

No apostrophe is needed in the possessive pronoun its.

it's = it is or it has	its = belonging to it

Relative pronouns

Relative pronouns are pronouns that relate back to something
or someone already mentioned.

that which
who whose

Usually, **who** is used to refer to people;
that or **which** is used to refer to animals
and objects.

> The man **who** likes cake is at the bakery.
> The cake **that** he likes has sold out.

Adjectives

An adjective tells you more about a noun or pronoun.

> The thief wore a **stripy** top, a **spotty** bandana, a **gold** earring and a **black** patch over one eye. He had a **colourful** parrot perched on his shoulder. Most notably, he had a **wooden** leg.

By adding the suffix -**er** or -**est** to an adjective, we can compare two or more nouns.

Adjective	Comparative adjective	Superlative adjective
rich	richer	richest
silly	sillier	silliest
small	smaller	smallest
young	younger	youngest
hairy	hairier	hairiest
clumsy	clumsier	clumsiest

Don't forget!

If you add -**er** or -**est** to a word ending in 'y', you change the 'y' to an 'i'.

frilly ⟶ frillier ⟶ frilliest

In one-syllable words with a short vowel sound, you usually need to double the final consonant before adding -**er** or -**est**.

fat ⟶ fatter ⟶ fattest

Some adjectives sound awkward if you add -**er** or -**est** to them.
We often put **more** or **most** in front of these instead.

Adjective	Comparative adjective	Superlative adjective
exciting	more exciting	most exciting
popular	more popular	most popular
beautiful	more beautiful	most beautiful

As always, there are exceptions! Several commonly used adjectives
do not follow the usual patterns...

Comparative injuries

bad   worse   worst

Comparative results

good   better   best

Determiners

Determiners pinpoint nouns, answering questions such as which, whose or how many?

a   the   my   some   every   your   fifty   this   those

Articles

The articles a, an and the are the most common type of determiner.

I found **a** hat in **an** old suitcase in **the** attic.

There are two types of article.

The definite article: **'the'** is a definite article because it refers to a specific thing.

I would like **the** cake with pink icing.

(This 'the' pinpoints exactly which cake I would like.)

The indefinite article: **'a'** or **'an'** are indefinite articles because they do not refer to a specific thing.

I would like **a** cake with my drink.

(This 'a' does not make clear which cake I would like.)

'A' and **'an'** mean the same thing but **'an'** is used before any word that starts with a vowel sound. It makes it easier to say.

A horse and **an** elephant danced for **an** hour.

Verbs

Verbs are sometimes called 'doing words' as they often describe an action.

skate

run

climb

kiss

knit

Not all verbs describe actions that can be seen. For example, some verbs refer to feelings.

I **love** my cat.

Verbs can also show what someone or something is or has.

It **is** cold outside.

I **have** two grandchildren.

Imperative verbs ('bossy' verbs) are used to instruct or give orders.

Eat your greens!
Wash your hands!
Be quiet!

Weigh the ingredients.
Place the ingredients in a bowl.
Mix well for two minutes.

Auxiliary and modal verbs

Auxiliary verbs ('helper' verbs) support other verbs, helping to show that something has happened, is happening, might or will happen.

I **am** climbing a tree.   I **have** knitted a scarf.   I **will** marry you!

Auxiliary verbs change form depending on who or what is the subject of the sentence, and when the action takes place. For example:

I **am** dancing. He **is** singing. She **is** eating. They **are** drinking. We **are** partying!

Modal verbs are a special kind of 'helper' verb. They support main verbs, often showing whether something is possible, allowed or likely.

shall could would
may must might
can will ought to
should

You will go to the ball!

I might dance with the prince!

Verb tenses

We modify verbs to make it clear when
something happens. The different verb forms
for past, present and future are called tenses.

Past	Present	Future
I ate carrots I have eaten carrots	I eat carrots I am eating carrots	I shall eat carrots I shall be eating carrots

Lots of present tense verbs can be changed into past tense verbs by adding
the suffix -ed.

talk ⟶ talked   yawn ⟶ yawned   jump ⟶ jumped

Grammar would be so much easier if all past tense verbs ended in -ed.
But the English language is full of lots of irregular verbs.

English verbs do not have special future tense
forms. Instead, we use the present tense verb form
and show the future tense with the help of an
auxiliary verb (e.g. shall or will).

Subject or object?

Every sentence has at least one subject noun and verb. It may also have an object noun. The subject noun is the person or thing doing the action. The object noun is usually on the receiving end of the action. The verb tells us what that person or thing is doing.

subject   verb   object

The dentist cleaned my teeth.

Subject and verb agreement

The subject and verb must agree. This means using the correct verb form to match the subject noun.

I agree!

He agrees!

We agree!

Grandma **plays** bingo on Fridays.   We **play** football after school.
Grandma **likes** bingo.   We **like** football.

Verbs change form depending on who or what is the subject of the sentence, and when the action takes place. Some irregular verbs, such as 'to be', have many different forms.

Present	Past
I am	I was
you are	you were
he/she is	he/she was
it is	it was
we are	we were
they are	they were

To be or not to be?

The prisoners be ready to walk the plank, Captain!

ARE!

The irregular verb 'to have' also has different forms.

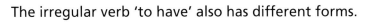

Child: I ain't got a pen.
Teacher: No! You **have** not got a pen; I **have** not got a pen; she **has** not got a pen; he **has** not got a pen; they **have** not got a pen.
Child: So where are all the pens?

Active and passive

Every sentence has a subject and a verb.
In sentences where the subject noun carries out
the action, the active voice is being used. In passive
voice sentences, the subject noun has an action
done to it by something or someone else.

subject

Active voice:

object

The dog stole my dinner.

subject

Passive voice:

object

My dinner was stolen by the dog.

In this sentence, Grandma (the subject of the sentence) has done the action
of baking. Therefore the active voice is being used.

Grandma baked a cake.

In this sentence, the order of the words has been changed. The passive voice is
being used. The meaning is the same but the cake is now the main focus (subject)
of the sentence.

A cake was baked by Grandma.

Most of the time we use the active
voice because the passive voice can
sound awkward.

Active

Passive

Grandma walked the dog.   **The dog was walked by Grandma.**

However, the passive voice can be effective in some formal writing.

For example:

A letter of complaint: The potatoes were undercooked.

A report: The suspect was seen running from the crime scene.

A formal notice: Children must be supervised at all times.

Active or passive?

It's not always easy to spot whether a sentence uses the active or passive voice, especially if it's unclear who or what has carried out the action. A trick that often helps is to first identify the verb, then add the phrase 'by Grandma' (or any character of your choice) immediately after it. If the sentence makes grammatical sense, it is likely to be passive. This trick won't always work, but it will help for lots of sentences!

The window was broken …

The cakes were burned …

The postman was frightened … **by Grandma**

We are being eaten …

Don't blame me for everything!

Adverbs

Most adverbs add to a verb, telling us more about how something is done.

The boy ran.   **The boy ran quickly.**

Lots of adjectives can be changed into adverbs by adding the suffix -**ly**.

quiet ⟶ **quietly**   slow ⟶ **slowly**   soft ⟶ **softly**

Sometimes an adverb is used to tell us more about an adjective or adverb.

The haunted house was quite scary.

The adverb 'quite' tells us more
about the adjective 'scary': it tells us
how scary the haunted house was.

Adverbials

An adverbial tells us more about a verb or clause. It can be a single adverb, phrase or subordinate clause. Adverbials provide additional information, explaining where, when, how or why something happens.

The skydiver jumped out of the plane **reluctantly**.   (single adverb)

The autograph hunters queued **for several hours**.   (adverbial phrase)

I let the dog out **when it started barking**.   (adverbial clause)

Fronted adverbials

A fronted adverbial is an adverb or adverbial that begins a sentence. It tells us more about an action that follows. Like any adverbial, it describes where, when, how or why something happens.

Don't forget! A comma is usually needed after a fronted adverbial.

After we had eaten, we watched TV.

Limping, the injured striker left the pitch.

Fronted adverbials can be a useful way to vary your sentence openers.

I go to Chess Club every Tuesday. ⟶ **Every Tuesday, I go to Chess Club.**

I go swimming to help me keep fit. ⟶ **To help me keep fit, I go swimming.**

I hug my teddy when I am scared. ⟶ **When I am scared, I hug my teddy.**

Prepositions

A preposition shows how one thing is related to another. It shows how nouns or pronouns are connected. There are lots of prepositions to describe the physical position of something or someone.

under	over	next to	in	below
in front of	after	up	down
above	on	beside	behind	far from
through	at

There's a boy **in** my soup!

How to spot a preposition...

Lots of prepositions are 'position' words.

A preposition is always followed by a noun, pronoun or noun phrase.

Lots of prepositions explain where or when things happen.

> My hamster likes to hide **under** my bed.
> The film starts **at** six o'clock.

Prepositions do not link clauses; that's a job for a conjunction.

Conjunctions

A conjunction is a 'linking' word. Its main job is to link different parts of a sentence. There are two main types of conjunction: coordinating conjunctions and subordinating conjunctions.

Coordinating conjunctions link two words, phrases or clauses that are equally important.

and but so or

A zebra has black and white stripes.

The conjunction 'and' links the words 'black' and 'white'.
The words 'black' and 'white' are of equal importance.

I enjoy watching quiz shows but **I hardly ever know the answers.**

The conjunction 'but' joins a pair of clauses. Each clause makes sense on its own, but the conjunction adds cohesion, helping the words to flow smoothly.

Subordinating conjunctions are used to introduce a subordinate clause.

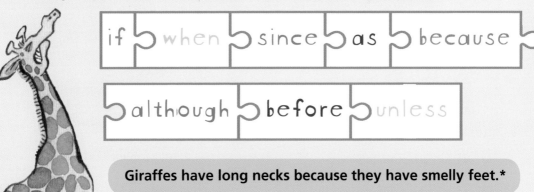

if when since as because

although before unless

Giraffes have long necks because they have smelly feet.*

The subordinating conjunction 'because' introduces the subordinate clause: 'because they have smelly feet'.
A subordinate clause does not make sense on its own.

*Giraffes don't really have smelly feet. Not unless they have stepped in something smelly.

Grandma's guide to different sentence types

Commands

A command is a sentence that gives an instruction or an order.
A command sometimes ends with an exclamation mark.

Eat your greens!

Statements

A statement is a sentence that gives information.
The information could be a fact or an opinion.
A statement usually ends with a full stop.

**You'll catch a chill if you go
out without your coat.**

Questions

A question is a sentence that asks something. It usually
requires an answer. A question ends with a question mark.

Have you washed your hands?

A rhetorical question is a special kind of question that does not require
an answer. Rhetorical questions can be effective in persuasive writing.

Who wouldn't enjoy a luxury holiday?

Exclamations

An exclamation is a sentence that expresses emotion, excitement or strong feeling. It ends with an exclamation mark.

I've won!

Interjections

An interjection is a word that expresses a warning, exclamation or short burst of emotion. It usually ends with an exclamation mark.

| Hey! | Phew! | Hooray! | Wow! | Eek! |

Words that represent a pause or hesitation are also interjections.

Why haven't you done your homework?

Um...

Er...

Well...

Phrases

A phrase is a small group of words that add to a single word. A phrase does not usually have a verb and doesn't make sense without the rest of the sentence.

Different kinds of phrases do different jobs. For example:

A noun phrase is a group of words that function as a noun or pronoun. The phrase expands on the noun, giving extra information.

the new sofa

a fluffy little kitten

my daft uncle

the man in the moon

a pink elephant

How to spot...

a noun phrase

If a phrase can be replaced with a pronoun (e.g. he, she, it), it is a noun phrase.

A preposition phrase has a preposition at its head. Most preposition phrases explain where something is. A preposition is always followed by a noun, pronoun or noun phrase.

over the road

under the sea

behind the sofa

Clauses

Not to be confused with Santa Claus!

I'm a Claus, not a clause!

A clause is a group of words which forms all or part of a sentence.
A clause has a subject and a verb.

> **A bird flew into a library.**

A sentence can have one or more clauses.

> **Libraries are rarely burgled** as **thieves are afraid of a long sentence.**

Some clauses are more important than others. A main clause is a complete idea that makes sense on its own. A subordinate clause doesn't make complete sense on its own. It is dependent on a main clause to make sense.

> **A bird flew into a library** because he was looking for bookworms.

main clause =
most important bit

subordinate clause =
less important bit

Clauses, like phrases, can do the job of nouns, adjectives and adverbs in a sentence. They add detail.

Subordinate clauses

A subordinate clause can be used at the beginning, middle or end of a sentence.

Because she ran away from the ball, Cinderella never scored a goal.

The soldier, **who was in the library,** could not find a book on camouflage.

Birds fly south in winter **because it's too far to walk.**

They can be useful because they provide extra information and help you to structure sentences in different ways. We use them all the time without knowing it!

A subordinate clause usually begins with either a subordinating conjunction:

if even until because although even though provided that whereas before

or a relative pronoun:

which that whose who

A subordinate clause that starts with a relative pronoun is also known as a relative clause.

How to spot a subordinate clause...

A subordinate clause does not make sense on its own.

If you remove a subordinate clause, the sentence should still make sense.

Commas, dashes or brackets are often used to separate subordinate clauses from main clauses.

Subordinate clauses have fluffy tails.*

*The last point is not true. Subordinate clauses do not have tails of any kind.

Relative clauses

A relative clause begins with a relative pronoun.

who   that   which   whose

Like all clauses, a relative clause contains a subject and a verb.

Relative clauses give us extra information about something.

> **Lofty Longfellow scored 24 points.**

> **Lofty Longfellow, who was the tallest basketball player we had ever seen, scored 24 points.**

What do you call Santa's wife?

A relative Clause.

What do you call Santa's elves?

Subordinate Clauses.

Sentences

A sentence is a group of words that makes complete sense. A sentence always has at least one subject noun and a verb. It can have one or more clauses.

Simple sentences

A simple sentence has one independent clause.

> **Grandma likes pizzas.**

Simple sentences are not always short.

> **My dear old grandma likes eating cheesy pizzas every day.**

Short simple sentences are useful when you want to make a point clearly and concisely. A simple sentence can also be dramatic.

> **The pizza was burnt!**

Compound sentences

A compound sentence has two or more independent clauses joined with a conjunction or semi-colon. Each clause makes sense on its own.

> **Dogs like chasing cats** but **cats can climb trees.**

Complex sentences

A complex sentence has a main (independent) clause and a subordinate clause.
The subordinate clause is dependent on the main clause to make sense.

The subordinate clause can be at the beginning,
middle or end of a complex sentence.

If you want to be a great footballer, you should practise every day.

Emily Parker, who was a secret agent, followed the man in the bowler hat.

I go skateboarding every Saturday, even if it's raining.

Synonyms and antonyms

Synonyms are words that are similar in meaning.

Your homework is terrible. Awful. Dreadful. Dire. Appalling. Horrendous. Atrocious...

The best place to find synonyms is in a thesaurus.

What do you call a dinosaur with an extensive vocabulary?

A thesaurus.

Top tip!

When you use a thesaurus to look up a verb, you will find it listed under its simplest form (infinitive). For example, if you are trying to find synonyms for 'said', you will need to look up 'say'.

Take care when choosing synonyms – they often have different shades of meaning. It can be tricky choosing the word that fits your sentence best.

It's not frightening – it's terrifying!

Antonyms are words that have opposite meanings.

Some prefixes can be used to create antonyms.

un	+ happy	= unhappy
un	+ do	= undo
dis	+ like	= dislike
dis	+ appear	= disappear
mis	+ behave	= misbehave
non	+ sense	= nonsense
anti	+ clockwise	= anticlockwise

Language effects
Alliteration, onomatopoeia, similes, metaphors and personification

Writers use different techniques to add richness to their writing.

Alliteration is when two or more words with the same initial sound are used close together.

Alliteration is often used in poetry.

> **The battered boat battled against the brutal waves.**

Alliteration can also be effective when used in other sorts of writing, such as song lyrics, stories, newspaper headlines or advertisements.

GOLDEN GIRL GUZZLES GRIZZLY BEARS' GRUB!

Onomatopoeia is when a word is used that imitates the sound it describes. Onomatopoeic words are sometimes called 'sound words'.

BOOM! WHOOSH CLICK BUZZ THUD! SPLASH CRASH!

Lots of animal sounds are examples of onomatopoeia.

MOO! TWEET! BARK! RIBBIT!

Similes compare two things by pointing out a similarity. They often use the words 'like' or 'as' to make a comparison.

Metaphors also make comparisons but a metaphor says that one thing *is* something else, without using the word 'like' or 'as'.

The ogre had large grey teeth like tombstones.

His feet were as cold as ice.

The village was hidden beneath a blanket of snow.

Life is a roller coaster.

Metaphors can also be used to describe people.

My little brother is a monster.

My teacher is a dragon.

Personification is when you give human characteristics to something that is not human.

The traffic slowed to a crawl.

A storm raged.

Common confusions

Fewer sprouts please, Grandma!

Less or fewer?

Nouns can be countable or non-countable.

For example:

> You can count oranges but you can't count juice.

> You can count sausages but you can't count gravy.

Use fewer for countable nouns.
Use less for non-countable nouns.

Their, they're or there?

Getting in a muddle with these same-sounding words can seem like a spelling problem. But your knowledge of grammar and punctuation can help you!

Their is a possessive determiner (see p22). It means 'belonging to them'.	They're is a contraction (see p12). It is short for 'they are'.	There is related to 'here'.
my	I'm (I am)	
your	you're (you are)	
our	he's (he is)	
his	she's (she is)	
her	it's (it is)	
its	we're (we are)	
their	they're (they are)	

HERE THERE

I or me?

In formal writing, the easiest way to choose between 'I' and 'me' in a sentence is to remove any other characters.

For example:

> **My grandson and me had an ice cream.**

or

> **My grandson and I had an ice cream.**

Where's my ice cream?

If I remove 'my grandson' from the sentence, it is easier to work out which is correct.

> **Me had an ice cream.**

> **I had an ice cream.**

Your or you're?

Confusing 'your' and 'you're' is not a spelling problem. Understanding that one is a possessive and the other is short for 'you are' should help you remember the difference.

Possessive determiners	Contractions	
my	I'm	(I am)
your	you're	(you are)
our	he's	(he is)
his	she's	(she is)
her	it's	(it is)
its	we're	(we are)
their	they're	(they are)

Its or it's?

When is an apostrophe needed?

An apostrophe should only be used in 'it's' when you are using a contraction, meaning 'it is'. If you are using 'its' as a possessive (meaning 'belonging to it'), no apostrophe is needed.

Index